Testament of Flamel

and

Other Works

Being a

Collection

on the

Sacred Art and Science

of

Alchemy

Nicholas Flamel

I

Testament of Nicholas Flamel

1. I Nicholas Flamel, a scrivener of Paris, in the year 1414, in the reign of our gracious Prince Charles the VIth, whom God preserve; and after the death of my faithful partner Perenelle, am seized with a desire and a delight, in remembrance of her, and in your behalf, dear nephew, to write out the whole magistery of the secret of the Powder of Projection, or the Philosophical Tincture, which God hath willed to impart to his very insignificant servant, and which I have found out, as thou also wilt find out in working as I shall declare unto you.

2. And for this cause do not forget to pray to God to bestow on thee the understanding of the reason of the truth of nature, which thou wilt see in this book, wherein I have written the secrets word for word, sheet by sheet, and also as I have done and wrought with thy dear aunt Perenelle, whom I very much regret.

3. Take heed before thou workest, to seek the right way as a man of understanding. The reason of nature is Mercury, Sun and Moon, as I have said in my book, in which are those figures which thou seest under the arches of the Innocents at Paris. But I erred greatly upwards of 23 years and a half, in labouring without being able to marry the Moon, that is quicksilver, to the Sun, and to extract from them the seminal dung, which is a deadly poison; for I was then ignorant of the agent or medium, in order to fortify the Mercury: for without this agent, Mercury is as common water.

4. Know in what manner Mercury is to be fortified by a metallic agent, without which it never can penetrate into the belly of the Sun and of the Moon; afterward it must be hardened, which cannot be affected without the sulphureous spirit of gold or silver. You must therefore first open them with a metallic agent, that is to say with royal Saturnia, and afterward you must actuate the Mercury by a philosophic means, that you may afterward by this Mercury dissolve into a liquor gold and Luna, and draw from their putrefaction the generative dung.

5. And know thou, that there is no other way nor means to work in this art, than that which I give thee word for word; an operation, unless it be taught as I now do, not at all easy to perform, but which on the contrary is very difficult to find out.

6. Believe stedfastly, that the whole philosophic industry consists in the preparation of the Mercury of the wise, for in it is the whole of

what we are seeking for, and which has always been sought for by all ancient wise men; and that we, no more than they, have done nothing without this Mercury, prepared with Sun or Moon: for without these three, there is nothing in the whole world capable of accomplishing the said philosophical and medicinal tincture. It is expedient then that we learn to extract from them the living and spiritual seed.

7. Aim therefore at nothing but Sun, Moon and Mercury prepared by a philosophical industry, which wets not the hands, but the metal, and which has in itself a metallic sulphureous soul, namely, the ignited light of sulphur. And in order that you may not stray from the right path, apply yourself to metals; for there the aforesaid sulphur is found in all; but thou wilt easily find it, even almost similar to gold, in the cavern and depths of Mars, which is iron, and of Venus, which is copper, nearly as much in the one as in the other; and even if you pay attention to it, this sulphur has the power of tinging moist and cold Luna, which is fine silver, into pure yellow and good Sun; but this ought to be done by a spiritual medium, viz. the key which opens all metals, which I am going to make known to you. Learn therefore, that among the minerals there is one which is a thief, and eats up all except Sun and Moon, who render the thief very good; for when he has them in his belly, he is good to prepare the quicksilver, as I shall presently make known to you.

8. Therefore do not stray out of the right road, but trust to my words, and then give thyself up to the practice, which I am going to bestow on thee in the name of the Father, of Son, and Holy Ghost.

The Practice.

9. Take thou in the first place the eldest or first-born child of Saturn, not the vulgar, 9 parts; of the sabre chalibs of the God of War, 4 parts. Put this latter into a crucible, and when it comes to a melting redness, cast therein the 9 parts of Saturn, and immediately this will redden the other. Cleanse thou carefully the filth that arises on the surface of the saturnia, with saltpetre and tartar, four or five times. The operation will be rightly done when thou seest upon the matter an astral sign like a star.

10. Then is made the key and the sabre, which opens and cuts through all metals, but chiefly Sun, Moon and Venus, which it eats, devours and keeps in his belly, and by this means thou art in the right road of truth, if thou has operated properly. For this Saturnia is the royal triumphant herb, for it is a little imperfect king, whom we raise up by a philosophic artifice to the degree of the greatest glory and honour.

It is also the queen, that is to say the Moon and the wife of the Sun: it is therefore both male and female, and our hermaphrodite Mercury. This Mercury or Saturnia is represented in the seven first pages of the book of Abraham the Jew, by two serpent encircling a golden rod. Take care to prepare a sufficient quantity of it, for much is required, that is to say about 12 or 13 lbs. of it, or even more, according as you wish to work on a large or a small scale.

11. Marry thou therefore the young god Mercury, that is to say quicksilver with this which is the philosophic Mercury, that you may acuate by him and fortify the said running quicksilver, seven or even ten or eleven times with the said agent, which is called the key, or a steel sharpened sabre, for it cuts, scythes and penetrates all the bodies of the metals. Then wilt thou have the double and treble water represented by the rose tree in the book of Abraham the Jew, which issues out of the foot of an oak, namely our Saturnia, which is the royal key, and goes to precipitate itself into the abyss, as says the same author, that is to say, into the receiver, adapted to the neck of the retort, where the double Mercury throws itself by means of a suitable fire.

12. But here are found thorns and insuperable difficulties, unless God reveals this secret, or a master bestows it. For Mercury does not marry with royal Saturnia: it is experient to find a secret means to unite them: for unless thou knowest the artifice by which this union and peace are effected between these aforesaid argent-vives, you will do nothing to any purpose. I would not conceal any thing from thee, my dear nephew; I tell thee, therefore, that without Sun or Moon this work will profit thee nothing. Thou must therefore cause this old man, or voracious wolf, to devour gold or silver in the weight and measure as I am now about to inform thee. Listen therefore to my words, that thou mayest not err, as I have done in this work. I say, therefore, that you must give gold to our old dragon to eat. Remark how well you ought to operate. For if you give but little gold to the melted Saturnia, the gold is indeed opened, but the quicksilver will not take; and here is an incongruity, which is not at all profitable. I have a long while and greatly laboured in this affliction, before I found out the means to succeed in it. If therefore you give him much gold to devour, the gold will not indeed be so much opened nor disposed, but then it will take the quicksilver, and they will both marry. Thus the means is discovered. Conceal this secret, for it is the whole, and neither trust it to paper, or to any thing else which may be seen. For we should become the cause of

great mischief. I give it thee under the seal of secrecy and of thy conscience, for the love I bear thee.

13. Take thou ten ounces of the red Sun, that is to so say, very fine, clean and purified nine or ten times by means of the voracious wolf alone: two ounces of the royal Saturnia; melt this in a crucible, and when it is melted, cast into it the ten ounces of fine gold; melt these two together, and stir them with a lighted charcoal. Then will thy gold be a little opened. Pour it on a marble slab or into an iron mortar, reduce it to a powder, and grind it well with three pounds of quicksilver. Make them to curd like cheese, in the grinding and working them to and fro: wash this amalgama with pure common water until it comes out clear, and that the whole mass appears clear and white like fine Luna. The conjunction of the gold with the royal golden Saturnia is effected, when the mass is soft to the touch like butter.

14. Take this mass, which thou wilt gently dry with linen or fine cloth, with great care: this is our lead, and our mass of Sun and Moon, not the vulgar, but the philosophical. Put it into a good retort of crucible earth, but much better of steel. Place the retort in a furnace, and adapt a receiver to it: give fire by degrees. Two hours after encrease your fire so that the Mercury may pass into the receiver: this Mercury is the water of the blowing rose-tree; it is also the blood of the innocents slain in the book of Abraham the Jew. You may now suppose that this Mercury has eat up a little of the body of the king, and that it will have much more strength to dissolve the other part of it hereafter, which will be more covered by the body of the Saturnia. Thou has now ascended one degree or step of the ladder of the art.

15. Take the faeces out of the retort; melt them in a crucible in a strong fire: cast into it four ounces of the Saturnia, (and) nine ounces of the Sun. Then the Sun is expanded in the said faeces, and much more opened that at the first time, as the Mercury has more vigour than before, it will have the strength and virtue of penetrating the gold, and of eating more of it, and of filling his belly with it by degrees. Operate therefore as at first; marry the aforesaid Mercury, stronger one degree with this new mass in grinding the whole together; they will take like butter and cheese; wash and grind them several times, until all the blackness is got out: dry it as aforesaid; put the whole into the retort, and operate as thou didst before, by giving during two hours, a weak fire, and then strong, sufficient to drive out, and cause the Mercury to fall into the receiver; then wilt thou have the Mercury still more

acuated, and thou wilt have ascended to the second degree of the philosophic ladder.

16. Repeat the same work, by casting in the Saturnia in due weight, that is to say, by degrees, and operating as before, till thou hast reached the 10th step of the philosophic ladder; then take thy rest. For the aforesaid Mercury is ignited, acuated, wholly engrossed and full of the male sulphur, and fortified with the astral juice which was in the deep bowels of the gold and of our saturnine dragon. Be assured that I am now writing for thee things which by no philosopher was ever declared or written. For this Mercury is the wonderful caduceus, of which the sages have so much spoken in their books, and which they attest has the power of itself of accomplishing the philosophic work, and they say the truth, as I have done it myself by it alone, and thou wilt be enabled to do it thyself, if thou art so disposed: for it is this and none else which is the proximate matter and the root of all the metals.

17. Now is done and accomplished the preparation of the Mercury, rendered cuting and proper to dissolve into its nature gold and silver, to work out naturally and simply the Philosophic Tincture, or the powder transmuting all metals into gold and silver.

18. Some believe they have the whole magistery, when they have the heavenly Mercury prepared; but they are grossly deceived. It is for this cause they find thorns before they pluck the rose, for want of understanding. It is true indeed, that were they to understand the weight, the regimen of the fire, and the suitable way, they would not have much to do, and could not fail even if they would. But in this art there is a way to work. Learn therefore and observe well how to operate, in the manner I am about to relate to you.

19. In the name of God, thou shalt take of thy animated Mercury what quantity thou pleasest; thou wilt put it into a glass vessel by itself; or two or four parts of the Mercury with two parts of the golden Saturnia; that is to say, one of the Sun and two of the Saturnia; the whole finely conjoined like butter, washed, cleansed and dried; and thou wilt lute thy vessel with the lute of wisdom. Place it in a furnace on warm ashes at the degree of the heat of an hen sitting on her eggs. Leave this said Mercury so prepared to ascend and descend for the space of 40 or 50 days, until thou seest forming in thy vessel a white or red sulphur, called philosophic sublimate, which issues out of the reins of the said Mercury. Thou wilt collect this sulphur with a feather: it is the living Sun and the living Moon, which Mercury begets out of itself.

20. Take this white or red sulphur, triturate it in a glass or marble mortar, and pour on it, in sprinking it, a third part of its weight of the Mercury from which this sulphur has been drawn. With these two make a paste like butter: put again this mixture into an oval glass; place it in a furnace on a suitable fire of ashes, mild, and disposed with a philosophic industry. Concoct until the said Mercury is changed into sulphur, and during this coction, thou wilt see wonderful things in thy vessel, that is to say, all the colours which exist in the world, which thou canst not behold without lifting up thy heart to God in gratitude for so great a gift.

21. When thou has attained to the purple red, thou must gather it: for then the alchymical powder is made, transmuting every metal into fine pure and neat gold, which thou maist multiply by watering it as thou hast already done, grinding it with fresh Mercury, concocting it in the same vessel, furnace and fire, and the time will be much shorter, and its virtue ten times stronger.

22. This then is the whole magistery done with Mercury alone, which some do not believe to be true, because they are weak and stupid, and not at all able to comprehend this work.

23. Shouldest thou desire to operate in another way, take of fine Sun in fine powder or in very thin leaves: make a paste of it with 7 parts of thy philosophic Mercury, which is our Luna: put them both into an oval glass vessel well luted; place it in a furnace; give a very strong fire, that is to say, such as will keep lead in fusion; for then thou has found out the true regimen of the fire; and let thy Mercury, which is the philosophical wind, ascend and descend on the body of the gold, which it eats up by degrees, and carries in its belly. Concoct it until the gold amd Mercury do no more ascend and descend, but both remain quiet, and then will peace and union be effected between the two dragons, which are fire and water both together.

24. Then wilt thou see in thy vessel a great blackness like that of melted pitch, which is the sign of the death and putrefaction of the gold, and the key of the whole magistery. Cause it therefore to resuscitate by concocting it, and be not weary with concocting it: during this period divers changes will take place; that is to say, the matter will pass through all the colours, the black, the ash colour, the blue, the green, the white, the orange, and finally the red as red as blood or the crimson poppy: aim only at this last colour; for it is the true sulphur, and the alchymical powder. I say nothing precisely about the time; for

that depends on the industry of the artist; but thou canst not fail, by working as I have shewn.

25. If thou are disposed to multiply thy powder, take one part thereof, and water it with two parts of thy animated Mercury; make it into a soft and smooth paste; put it in a vessel as thou hast already done, in the same furnace and fire, and concoct it. This second turn of the philosophic wheel will be done in less time than the first, and thy powder will have ten times more strength. Let is wheel about again even a thousand times, and as much as thou wilt. Thou wilt then have a treasure without price, superior to all there is in the world, and thou canst desire nothing more here below, for thou hast both health and riches, if thou useth them properly.

26. Thou hast now the treasure of all worldly felicity, which I a poor country clown of Pointoise did accomplish three times in Paris, in my house, in the street des Ecrivains, near the chapel of St. Jacques de la Boucherie, and which I Flammel give thee, for the love I bear thee, to the honour of God, for His glory, for the praise of Father, Son, and Holy Spirit. Amen.

The French correspondent [who had provided the French version to the editor for translation into English for this publication of 1806] adds: "This is what I find at the end of the Manuscript"'

They assert that the original of this work was written upon the margin of a vellum Psalm-book, in Nicholas Flamel's own handwriting in favour of his nephew. The process was written in cyphers, the better to conceal the secret. Each letter was shaped in four different ways, so that to make up the whole alphabet therewith 96 letters were employed. Father Pernetti and Monsieur de Saint Marc decyphered this writing with much difficulty. M. de St. Marc was on the point of giving it up; but Father Pernetti, who had already found out the vowels, encouraged him to go on with the work, which they at last overcame, with complete success, about the year 1758.

The Summary of Philosophy

If you would know how metals are transmuted, you must understand from what matter they are generated, and how they are formed in the mines; and that you may not err, you must see and observe, how those transmutations are performed in the bowels or veins of the earth.

Minerals taken out of the earth, may be changed, if beforehand they be spiritualized, and reduced into their sulphureous and argent vive nature, which are the two sperms, composed of the elements, the one masculine, the other feminine. - The male sulphur, is nothing but fire and air; and the true sulphur is as a fire, but not the vulgar, which contains no metallic substance. The feminine sperm is argent vive, which is nothing but earth and water; these two sperms the ancient sages called two dragons or serpents, of which, the one is winged, the other not. Sulphur not flying the fire, is without wings; the winged serpent is argent vive, borne up by the wind, therefore in her certain hour she flies from the fire, not having fixity enough to endure it. Now if these two sperms, separated from themselves, be united again, by powerful nature, in the potentiality of mercury, which is the metallic fire: being thus united, it is called by the philosophers the flying dragon; - because the dragon kindled by its fire, while he flies by little and little, fills the air with his fire, and poisonous vapours. - The same thing doth mercury; for being placed upon an exterior fire, and in its place in a vessel; it sets on fire its inside, which is hidden in its profundity; by which may be seen, how the external fire does burn and inflame the natural mercury. - And then you may see how the poisonous vapour breaks out into the air, with a most stinking and pernicious poison; which is nothing else but the head of the dragon, which hastily goes out of Babylon. But other philosophers have compared this mercury, with a flying lion, because a lion is a devourer of other creatures, and delights himself in his voracity of every thing, except that which is able to resist his violence and fury. So also does mercury, which has in itself such a power, force, and operation, to spoil and devastate a metal of its form, and to devour it. Mercury being too much influenced, devours and hides metals in its belly; but which of them so ever it be, it is certain, that, it consumes it not, for in their nature they are perfect, and much more indurate. But mercury has in itself a substance of perfecting sol and luna; and all the imperfect bodies or metals, proceed from argent vive; therefore the ancients called it the mother of metals; whence it follows, that in its own principle and centre, being formed, it has a double metallic substance. And first, the substance of the interior; then the substance of sol, which is not like the other metals; of these two substances, argent vive is formed, which in its body is spiritually nourished. As soon then as nature has formed argent vive, of the two after-named spirits, then it endeavors to make them perfect and corporeal; but when the spirits are of strength, and the two sperms awakened out of their central principle, then they desire to assume their own bodies. Which being done, argent vive the mother must die, and being thus naturally mortified, cannot (as dead things cannot) quicken itself as before. But there are some proud philosophers, who in obscure words affirm, that we ought to transmute both perfect and imperfect bodies into running argent vive; this is the serpent's subtlety, and you may be in danger of being bit by it. It is true, that argent vive may transmute an imperfect body, as lead or tin; and may without much labour, multiply in a quantity; but thereby it diminishes or loses its own perfection, and may no more for this reason be called argent vive. But if by art it may be mortified, that it can no more vivify itself, then it will be changed into another thing, as in cinnabar, or sublimate is done. For when it is by the art coagulated, whether sooner or later, yet then its two bodies assume not a fixed body, nor can they conserve it, as we may see in the bowels of the earth.

Lest anyone should therefore err, there are in the veins of lead some fixed grains or particles of fine sol and luna mixed in its substance of nourishment.

The first coagulation of argent vive is in the mine of saturn; and most fit and proper it is to bring him unto perfection and fixation; for the mine of saturn is not without fixed particles of gold, which particles were imparted to it by nature. So in itself it may be multiplied and brought to perfection, and a vast power or strength, as I have tried, and therefore affirm it.- So long as it is not separated from its mine, viz. its argent vive, but well kept, (for every metal which is in its mine, the same is an argent vive) then may it multiply itself, for that it has substance from its mercury, or argent vive, but it will be like some green immature fruit on a tree, which the blossom being past, becomes an unripe fruit, and then a larger apple. Now if any one plucks this unripe fruit from the tree, then its first forming would be frustrate, nor would it grow larger nor ripe; for man knows not how to give substance, nourishment, or maturity, so well as internal nature, while the fruit yet hangs on the tree, which feeds it with substance and nourishment, till the determined maturity is accomplished.

And so long also does the fruit draw sap or moisture for its augmentation and nourishment, till it comes to its perfect maturity. So is it with sol; for if by nature, a grain, or grains are made, and it is reduced to its argent vive, then also by the same it is daily, without ceasing, sustained and supplied, and reduced into its place, viz. argent vive, as he is in himself; and then must you wait till he shall obtain some substance from his mercury as it happens in the fruit of trees. For as the argent vive, both of perfect and imperfect bodies is a tree, so they can have no more nourishment, otherwise than from their own mercury.

If therefore you would gather fruits from argent vive, viz. pure sol and luna, if they be disjoined from their mercury; think not that you, like as nature did in the beginning, may again conjoin and multiply, and without change, augment them. For if metals be separated from their mine, then they, like the fruit of trees too soon gathered, never come to their perfection, as nature and experience makes it appear. For if an apple or pear be once plucked off from the tree, it would then be a great vanity to attempt to fasten it to the tree again, expecting it to encrease and grow ripe; and experience testifies, that the more it is handled, the more it withereth. And so it is also with metals: for if you should take the vulgar sol and luna, endeavoring to reduce them into argent vive, you would wholly play the fool, for there is no artifice yet found, whereby it can be performed. - Though you should use many waters, and cements, or other things infinitely of that kind, yet would you continually err, and that would befal you, which would him that should tie unripe fruit to their trees.

Yet some philosophers have said truly, that if sol and luna, by a right mercury, or argent vive be rightly conjoined, they will make all imperfect metals perfect; but in this thing most men have erred, who having these three vegetables, animals, and minerals, which in one thing are conjoined; for that they considered not, that the philosophers speak not of vulgar sol, luna, and mercury, which are all dead, and receive no more substance or increase from nature, but remain the same in their own essence, without the possibility of bringing others to perfection.

They are fruits plucked off from their trees before their time, and are therefore of no value or estimation. Therefore see the fruit in the tree, that leads them straight to it, whose fruit is daily made greater with increase, so long as the tree bears it. This work is seen with joy and satisfaction; and by this means one may transplant the tree without gathering the fruit, fixing it into a moister, better, and more fruitful place, which in one day will give more nourishment to the fruit, than it received otherwise in an hundred years.

In this therefore, it is understood, that mercury, the much commended tree must be taken, which has in its power indissolvably sol and luna; and then transplanted into another soil nearer the sun, that thence it may gain its profitable increase, for which thing, dew does abundantly suffice; for where it was placed before, it was so weakened by cold and wind, that little fruit could be expected from it, and where it long stood and brought forth no fruit at all.

And indeed the philosophers have a garden, where the sun as well morning as evening remains with a moist sweet dew, without ceasing, with which it is sprinkled and moistened; - whose earth brings forth trees and fruits, which are transplanted thither, which also receive descent and nourishment from the pleasant meadows. And this is done daily, and there they are both corroborated and quickened, without ever fading; and this more in one year, than in a thousand, where the cold affects them. - Take them therefore, and night and day cherish them in a distillatory fire; but not with a fire of wood or coals, but in a clear transparent fire, not unlike the sun, which is never hotter than is requisite, but is always alike; for a vapour is the dew, and seed of metals, which ought not to be altered.

Fruits, if they be too hot, and without dew or moisture, they abide on the boughs, but without coming to perfection, only withering or dwindling away. But if they be fed with heat and due moisture on their trees, then they prove elegant and fruitful; for heat and moisture are the elements of all earthly things, animal, vegetable, and mineral. Therefore fires of wood and coal produce or help not metals; those are violent fires, which nourish not as the heat of the sun does, that conserves all corporeal things; for that it is natural which they follow. But a philosopher acts not what nature does; for nature where she rules, forms all vegetables, animals, and minerals, in their own degrees. Men, do not after the same sort, by their arts make natural things. When nature has finished her work about them; then by our art they are made more perfect. - In this manner the ancient sages and philosophers, for our information, wrought on luna and mercury her true mother, of which they made the mercury of the philosophers, which in its operation is much stronger than the natural mercury. For this is serviceable only to the simple, perfect, imperfect, hot and cold metals; but our mercury, the philosophers stone, is useful to the more than perfect, imperfect bodies, or metals. Also that the sun may perfect and nourish them without diminution, addition, or immutation, as they were created or formed by nature, and so leave them, not neglecting any thing.

I will not now say, that the philosophers conjoin the tree, for the better perfecting their mercury, as some unskilful in the nature of things, and unlearned chemists affirm, who take common sol, luna, and mercury, and so unnaturally handle them, till they vanish in smoak. These men endeavor to make the philosophers mercury, but they never attain it, which is the first matter of the stone, and the first minera thereof. If you would come hither and find good, and to the mountain of the seaven, where there is no plain, you would betake yourself; from the highest, you must look downward to the sixth, which you will see afar off. In the height of this mountain, you will find a royal herb triumphing, which some have called mineral, some vegetable, some saturnine. But let its bones or ribs be left, and let a pure clean broth be taken from it, so will the better part of your work be done. This is the right and subtle mercury of the philosophers, which you are to take, which will make first the white work, and then the red. If you have well understood me, both of them are nothing else, as they term them, but the practice, which is so easy and simple, that a woman sitting by her distaff may perfect it. As if in winter she would put her eggs under a hen, and not wash them, because eggs are put under a hen without washing them, and no more labour is required about them, than that they should be every day turned, that the chickens may be the better and sooner hatched, concerning the which enough is said.

But that I may follow the example, first, wash not the mercury, but take it, and with its like, which is fire, place it in the ashes, which is straw, and in one glass which is the nest, without any other things in a convenient alembic, which is the house, from whence it will come forth a chicken, which with its blood will free thee from all diseases, and with its flesh will nourish thee, and with its feathers will clothe thee, and keep thee warm from the injuries of the cold and ambient air. For this cause I have written this present treatise, that you may search with the greater desire, and walk in the right way. And I have written this small book, this summary, that you might better comprehend the sayings and writings of the philosophers, which I believe you will much better understand for time to come.

The Explication of the Hieroglyphic Figures.

Placed by me, Nicholas Flammel, Scrivener, in the Church-yard of the Innocents, in the fourth Arch, entering by the great gate of St. Dennis Street, and taking the way on the right hand.

THE INTRODUCTION.

Although that I, Nicholas Flammel, Notary, and abiding in Paris, in this year one thousand three hundred fourscore and nineteen, and dwelling in my house in the street of Notaries, near unto the Chapel of St. James of the Bouchery; although, I say, that I learned but a little Latin, because of the small means of my Parents, which nevertheless were, by them that envy me the most, accounted honest people; yet by the grace of God, and the intercession of the blessed Saints in Paradise of both sexes, and principally of St. James of Gallicia,

I have not wanted the understanding of the Books of the Philosophers, and in them learned their so hidden secrets. And for this cause, there shall never be any moment of my life when I remember this high good, wherein upon my knees (if the place will give me leave), or otherwise, in my heart with all my affection, I shall not render thanks to this most benign God, which never suffereth the child of the just to beg from door to door, and deceiveth not them which wholly trust in his blessing.

Whilst, therefore, I Nicholas Flammel, Notary, after the decease of my Parents, got my living in our Art of Writing, by making Inventories, dressing accounts, and summing up the expenses of Tutors and Pupils, there fell into my hands for the sum of two florins, a guilded Book, very old and large. It was not of Paper, nor of Parchment, as other Books be, but was only made of delicate rinds (as it seemed unto me) of tender young trees. The cover of it was of brass, well bound, all engraven with letters, or strange figures; and for my part I think they might well be Greek Characters, or some-such-like ancient language. Sure I am, I could not read them, and I know well they were not notes nor letters of the Latin nor of the Gaul for of them we understand a little. As for that which was within it, the leaves of bark or rind, were engraven, and with admirable diligence written, with a point of Iron, in fair and neat Latin letters, coloured. It contained thrice-seven leaves, for so were they counted in the top of the leaves, and always every seventh leaf was without any writing; but, instead thereof, upon the first seventh leaf, there was painted a Rod and Serpents swallowing it up.

In the second seventh, a Cross where a Serpent was crucified;

and in the last seventh there were painted Deserts, or Wildernesses, in the midst whereof ran many fair fountains, from whence there issued out a number of Serpents, which ran up and down here and there.

Upon the first of the leaves was written in great Capital Letters of Gold: Abraham the Jew, Prince, Priest, Levite, Astrologer, and Philosopher, to the Nation of the Jews, by the Wrath of Cod dispersed among the Gauls, sendeth Health. After this it was filled with great execrations and curses (with this word Maranatha, which was often repeated there) against every person that should cast his eyes upon it if he were not Sacrificer or Scribe.

He that sold me this Book knew not what it was worth, no more than I when I bought it; I believe it had been stolen or taken from the miserable Jews; or found hid in some part of the ancient place of their abode. Within the Book, in the second leaf, he comforted his Nation, councelling them to fly vices, and above all, Idolatry, attending with sweet patience the coming of the Messias, who should vanquish all the Kings of the Earth, and should reign with his people in glory eternally. Without doubt this had been some very wise and understanding man. In the third leaf, and in all the other writings that followed, to help his Captive nation to pay their tributes unto the Roman Emperors, and to do other things, which I will not speak of, he taught them in common words the transmutation of Metals; he painted the Vessels by the sides, and he advertised them of the colours, and of all the rest, saving of the first agent, of the which he spake not a word; but only (as he said) in the fourth and fifth leaves entire he painted it, and figured it with very great cunning and workmanship: for although it was well and intelligibly figured and painted, yet no man could ever have been able to understand it without being well skilled in their Cabala, which goeth by tradition, and without having well studied their books. The fourth and fifth leaves therefore, were without any writing, all full of fair figures enlightened, or as it were enlightened, for the work was very exquisite. First, he painted a young men with wings at his ankles, having in his hand a Caducean rod, writhen about with two Serpents, wherewith he struck upon a helmet which covered his head.

He seemed to my small judgment, to be the God Mercury of the Pagans: against him there came running and flying with open wings, a great old man, who upon his head had an hour-glass fastened, and in his hand a hook (or scythe) like Death, with the which, in terrible and furious manner, he would have cut off the feet of Mercury. On the other side of the fourth leaf, he painted a fair flower on the top of a very high mountain, which was sore shaken with the North wind; it had the foot blue, the flowers white and red, the leaves shining like fine gold: and round about it the Dragons and Griffons of the North made their nests and abode.

On the fifth leaf there was a fair Rose-tree, flowered in the midst of a sweet Garden, climbing up against a hollow Oak;

at the foot whereof boiled a fountain of most white water, which ran head-long down into the depths, notwithstanding it first passed among the hands of infinite people, who digged in the earth seeking for it; but because they were blind, none of them knew it, except here and there one who considered the weight.

On the last side of the fifth leaf there was a King, with a great Fauchion, who made to be killed in his presence by some Soldiers a great multitude of little Infants, whose Mothers wept at the feet of the unpitiful Soldiers the blood of which Infants was afterwards by other Soldiers gathered up, and put in a great vessel, wherein the Sun and the Moon came to bathe themselves. And because that this History did represent the more part of that of the Innocents slain by Herod, and that in this Book I learned the greatest part of the Art, this was one of the causes why I placed in their Church-yard these Hieroglyphic Symbols of this secret science. And thus you see that which was in the first five leaves. I will not represent unto you that which was written in good and intelligible Latin in all the other written leaves, for God would punish me; because I should commit a greater wickedness than he who (as it is said) wished that all the men of the World had but one head, that he might cut it off with one blow. Having with me, therefore, this fair book, I did nothing else day nor night but study upon it, understanding very well all the operations that it showed, but not knowing with what Matter I should begin, which made me very heavy and solitary, and caused me to fetch many a sigh. My wife Perrenella, whom I loved as myself, and had lately married, was much astonished at this, comforting me, and earnestly demanding if she could by any means deliver me from this trouble. I could not possibly hold my tongue, but told her all, and showed this fair book, whereof at the same instant that she saw it, she became as much enamoured as myself, taking extreme pleasure to behold the fan cover, gravings, images, and portraits, whereof, notwithstanding she understood as little as I; yet it was a great comfort to me to talk with her, and to entertain myself, what we should do to have the interpretation of them. In the end I caused to be painted within my Lodging, as naturally as I could, all the figures and portraits of the fourth and fifth leaf, which I showed to the greatest Clerks in Paris, who understood thereof no more than myself: I told them they were found in a Book that taught the Philosophers' Stone, but the greatest part of them made a mock both of me and that blessed Stone, excepting one called Master Anselme, who was a Licentiate in Physic, and studied hard in this Science. He had a great desire to have seen my Book, and there was nothing in the world he would not have done for a sight of it: but I always told him I had it not; only I made him a large description of the Method. He told me that the first portrait represented Time, which devoured all; and that according to the number of the six written leaves, there was required the space of six years, to perfect the Stone; and then, he said, we must turn the glass, and seethe it no more. And when I told him that this was not painted, but only to show and teach the first agent, (as was said in the Book) he answered me that this decoction for six years space was, as it were, a second Agent; and that certainly the first Agent was there painted, which was the white and heavy water, which without doubt was Argent Vive, which they could not fix, nor cut off his feet, that is to say, take away his volatility, save by that long decoction in the purest blood of young Infants; for in that, this Argent Vive being joined with gold and Silver, was first turned with them into an herb like that which was there painted, and afterwards, by corruption, into Serpents; which Serpents being then wholly dried, and decocted by fire, were reduced into powder of gold, which should be the Stone. This was the cause that during the space of one and twenty years, I tried a thousand broulleryes, yet never with blood, for that was wicked and villaneous: for I found in my Book that the Philosophers called Blood the mineral spirit which is in the Metals, principally in the Sun, Moon, and Mercury, to the assembling whereof, I always tended; yet these interpretations for the most part were more subtil than true. Not seeing, therefore, in my works the signs at the time written in my Book, I was always to begin again. In the end, having lost all hope of ever understanding those figures, for my last refuge I made a vow to God and St. James of Gallicia, to demand the interpretation of them at some Jewish Priest in some Synagogue of Spain. whereupon, with the consent of Perrenella, carrying with me the Extract of the Pictures, having taken the Pilgrims' habit and staff, in the same fashion as you may see me without this same Arch, in the Church-yard in the which I put these Hieroglyphical Figures, where I have also set against the wall, on the one and the other side, a Procession, in which are represented by order all the colours of the Stone, so as they come and go, with this writing in French: Much pleaseth God procession, If it be done in devotion.

Which is as it were the beginning of King Hercules his Book, which entreateth of the colours of the Stone, entitled Iris, or the Rainbow, in these termes, The procession of the work: is very pleasant unto Nature: the which I have put there expressly for the great Clerks who shall understand the Allusion. In this same fashion, I say, I put myself upon my way; and so much I did that I arrived at Montjoy, and afterwards at St. James, where with great devotion I accomplished my vow. This done, in Leon, at my return, I met with a Merchant of Bologn, who made me known to a Physician, a Jew by Nation, and as then a Christian, dwelling in Leon aforesaid, who was very skilful in sublime Sciences, called Master Canches. As soon as I had shown him the figures of my Extract, he being ravished with great astonishment and joy, demanded of me incontinently if I could tell him any news of the Book from whence they were drawn! I answered him in Latin, (wherein he asked me the question) that I hoped to have some good news of the Book, if anybody could decipher unto me the Enigmas. All at that instant transported with great Ardor and joy, he began to decipher unto me the beginning. But to be short, he well content to learn news where this Book should be, and I to hear him speak; and certainly he had heard much discourse of the Book, but, (as he said) as of a thing which was believed to be utterly lost, we resolved of our voyage, and from Leon we passed to Oviedo, and from thence to Sansom, where we put ourselves to Sea to come into France. Our voyage had been fortunate enough, and all-ready since we were entered into this Kingdom he had most truly interpreted unto me the greatest part of my figures, where even unto the very points and pricks he found great mysteries, which seemed unto me wonderful; when arriving at Orleans, this learned man fell extremely sick, being afflicted with excessive vomitings, which remained still with him of those he had suffered at Sea, and he was in such a continual fear of my forsaking him that he could imagine nothing like unto it. And although I was always by his side, yet would he incessantly call for me; but, in sum, he died at the end of the seventh day of his sickness, by reason whereof I was much grieved; yet, as well as I could, I caused him to be buried in the Church of the Holy Cross at Orleans, where he yet resteth: God have his soul, for he died a good Christian. And surely, if I be not hindered by death, I will give unto that Church some revenue, to cause some Masses to be said for his soul every day. He that would see the manner of my arrival and the joy of Perrenella, let him look upon us two, in this City of Paris, upon the door of the Chapel of St. James of the Bouchery, close by the one side of my house, where we are both painted, myself giving thanks at the feet of St. James of Gallicia, and Perrenella at the feet of St. John, whom she had so often called upon. So it was that by the grace of God, and the intercession of the happy and holy Virgin, and the blessed Saints James and John, I knew all that I desired, that is to say, The first Principles, yet not their first preparation, which is a thing most difficult above all the things in the world. But in the end I had that also, after long errors of three years, or thereabouts; during which time I did nothing but study and labour, so as you may see me without this o4rch, where I have placed my Processions against the two Pillars of it, under the feet of St. James and St. John, praying always to God, with my Beads in my hand, reading attentively within a Book, and poysing the words of the Philosophers: and afterwards trying and proving the divers operations, which I imagined to myself by their only words. finally, I found that which I desired, which I also soon knew by the strong scent and odour thereof. Having this, I easily accomplished the Mastery, for, knowing the preparation of the first Agents, and after following my Book according to the letter, I could not have missed it, though I would. Then, the first time that I made projection was upon Mercury, whereof I turned half-a-pound, or thereabouts, into pure Silver, better than that of the Mine, as I myself assayed, and made others assay many times. This was upon a Monday, the 17th of January, about noon, in my house, Perrenella only being present, in the year of the restoring of mankind, 1382. And afterwards, following always my Book, from word to word, I made projection of the Red Stone upon the like quantity of Mercury, in the presence likewise of Perrenella only, in the same house, the five and twentieth day of April following, the same year, about five o'clock in the evening; which I transmuted truly into almost as much pure Cold, better assuredly than common Gold, more soft and more plyable. I may speak it with truth, I have made it three times, with the help of Perrenella, who understood it as well as I, because she helped in my operations, and without doubt, if she would have enterprised to have done it alone, she had attained to the end and perfection thereof. I had indeed enough when I had once done it, but I found exceeding great pleasure and delight in seeing and contemplating the Admirable works of Nature within the Vessels. To signify unto thee, then, how I have done it three times, thou shalt see in this Arch, if thou have any skill to know them, three furnaces, like unto them which serve for our operations, I was afraid a long time, that Perrenella could not hide the extreme joy of her felicity, which I measured by mine own, and lest she should let fall some word amongst her kindred of the great treasures which we possessed: for extreme joy takes away the understanding, as well as great heaviness; but the goodness of the most great God had not only filled me with this blessing, to give me a wife chaste and sage, for she was moreover, not only capable of reason, but also to do all that was reasonable, and more discrete and secret than ordinarily other women are. Above all, she was exceeding devout, and therefore, seeing herself without hope of children, and now well stricken in years, she began as I did, to think of God, and to give ourselves to the works of Mercy. At that time when I wrote this Commentary, in the year one thousand four hundred and thirteen, in the end of the year, after the decease of my faithful companion, which I shall lament all the days of my life; she and I had already founded, and endued with revenues, 14 Hospitals in this City of Paris, we had now built from the ground three Chapels, we had enriched with great gifts and good rents, seven Churches, with many reparations in their Churchyards, besides that which we have done at Bologne, which is not much less than that which we have done here. I will not speak of the good which both of us have done to particular poor folks, principally to widows and poor orphans, whose names if I should tell, and how I did it, besides that my reward should be given me in this World,

I should likewise do displeasure to those good persons, whom I pray God bless, which I would not do for anything in the World. Building, therefore, these Churches, Church-yards and Hospitals, in this City, I resolved myself, to cause to be painted in the fourth Arch of the Church-yard of the Innocents, as you enter in by the great gate in St. Dennis-street, and taking the way on the right hand, the most true and essential marks of the Art, yet under veils, and Hieroglyphical

27

covertures, in imitation of those which are in the guilded Book of Abraham the Jew, which may represent two things, according to the capacity and understanding of them that behold them: First, the mysteries of our future and undoubted Resurrection, at the day of Judgment, and coming of good Jesus (whom may it please to have mercy upon us), a History which is well agreeing to a Church-yard. And, secondly, they may signify to them, who are skilled in Natural Philosophy, all the principal and necessary operations of the Mastery. These Hieroglyphic figures shall serve as two ways to lead unto the heavenly life: the first and most open sense teaching the sacred Mysteries of our salvation; (as I will show hereafter) the other teaching every man that hath any small understanding in the Stone the lineary way of the work; which being perfected by any one, the change of evil into good takes away from him the root of all sin, (which is covetousness) making him liberal, gentle, pious, religious, and fearing God, how evil soever he was before, for from thenceforward he is continually ravished with the great grace and mercy which he hath obtained from God, and with the profoundness of his Divine and admirable works. These are the reasons which have moved me to set these forms in this fashion, and in this place, which is a Church-yard, to the end that if any man obtain this inestimable good, to conquer this rich golden Fleece, he may think with himself (as I did) not to keep the talent of God digged in the Earth, buying Lands and possessions, which are the vanities of this world: but rather to work charitably towards his brethren, remembering himself that he learned this secret amongst the bones of the dead, in whose number he shall shortly be found; and that after this life he must render an account before a just and redoubtable Judge, who will censure even to an idle and vain word. Let him, therefore, who having well weighed my words, and well known and understood my figures, hath first gotten elsewhere the knowledge of the first beginnings and Agents, (for certainly in these Figures and Commentaries he shall not find any step or information thereof), perfect, to the glory of God, the Mastery of Hermes, remembering himself of the Church Catholic, Apostolic, and Roman; and of all other Churches, Church-yards, and Hospitals; and above all of the Church of the Innocents in this City, (in the Church-yard whereof he shall have contemplated these true demonstrations); opening bounteously his purse to them that are secretly poor honest people, desolate, weak women, widows, and forlorn orphans. So be it.

CHAPTER I
Of the Theological Interpretations, which may be given to these Hieroglyphics, according to the sense of me the Author

I have given to this Churchyard, a Charnel-house, which is right over against this fourth Arch, in the middest of the Churchyard, and against one of the Pillars of this Charnel house, I have made be drawn with a coal, and grossly painted, a man all black, which looks straight upon these Hieroglyphics, about whom there is written in French: It voy merveile done moult Ie m'esbahi; that is, I see a marvel, whereat I am much amazed: This, as also three plates of Iron and Copper gilt, on the East, West, and South of the Arch, where these Hieroglyphics are, in the middest of the Churchyard representing the holy Passion and Resurrection of the Son of God this ought not to be otherwise interpreted, than according to the common Theological sense, saving that this black man, may as well proclaim it a wonder of God in the transmutation of Metals, which is figured in these Hieroglyphics, which he so attentively looks upon, as to see buried so many bodies, which shall rise again out of their Tombs at the fearful day of judgement. On the other part I do not think it needful to interpret in a Theological sense that vessel of Earth on the right hand of these figures, within the which there is a Pen and Inkhorn, or rather vessel of Phylosophy, if thou take away the strings, and join the Pen to the Inkhorne: nor the other two like it, which are on the two sides of the figures of Saint Peter, and Saint Paul, within one of the which, there is an N. which signifieth Nicholas, and within the other an F. which signifieth Flammel. For these vessels signify nothing else, but that in the like of them, I have done the Maistery three times. Moreover, he that will also believe that I have put these vessels in form of Scutchions to represent this Pen and Inkhorn, and the capital letters of my name, let him believe it if he will, because both these interpretations are true.

Neither must you interpret in a Theological sense that writing which followeth, in these terms, NICHOLAS FLAMEL ET PERRENELLE SA FEMME, that is, Nicholas Flammel, and Perrenelle his wife, in as much as that signifieth nothing, but that I and my wife have given that Arch.

As to the third, fourth, and fifth Tables following, by the sides whereof is written, COMMENT LES INNOCENTS FVRENTOCCIS PAR LE COMMANDEMENT DV ROY

HERODES, that is How the Innocents were killed by the commandment of King Herod. The theological sense is well enough understood by the writing, we must only speak of the rest, which is above.

The two Dragons united together to one within the other, of colour black and blue, in a field sable, that is to say, black, whereof the one hath the wings gilded, and the other hath none at all, are the sins which naturally are enserchayned, for the one hath his original and birth from another: Of them some may be easily chased away, as they come easily, for they fly towards us every hour; and those which have no wings can never be chased away, such as is the sin against the holy Ghost. The Gold which is in the wings signifieth that the greatest part of sins commeth from the unholy hunger after gold; which makes so many people diligently to harken from whence they may have it: and the colour black and blue showeth that these are the desires that come out of the dark pits of hell, which we ought wholly to fly from. These two Dragons may also morely represent unto us the Legions of evil spirits which are always about us, and which will accuse us, before the just judge, at the fearful day of Judgement, which do ask nor seek nothing else but to sist us.

The man and the woman which are next them, of an orange colour, upon a field azure and blue, signify that men and women ought not to have their hope in this World, for the orange colour intimates dispair, or the letting go of hope, as here; and the colour azure and blue, upon they are painted, shows us that we must think of heavenly things to come, and say as the roule of the man doth, HOMO VENIET ADIVICIVM DEI, that is, Man must come to the judgement of God may show mercy unto us.

Next after this in a field of Syneple, that is green, are painted two men and one woman rising again, of the which one comes out of a Sepulchre, the other two out of the Earth, all three of colour exceeding white and pure, lifting their hands towards their eyes, and their eyes towards Heaven on high: Above these three bodies there are two Angels sounding musical Instruments; as if they had called these dead to the day of Judgement; for over these two Angels is the figure of our Lord Jesus Christ, holding the world in his hand, upon whose head an Angel setteth a Crown, assisted by two others, which say in their roules, O pater Omnipotens, o'jesu bone, that is, O Father Almighty, O'good Jesu. On the right side of this Saviour is painted St. Paul, clothed with white & yellow, with a Sword, at whose feet there is a man clothed in a gown of orange colour, in which there appeared pleats or folds of black and white, (which picture resembleth me to the life) and demandeth pardon of his sins, holding his hands joined together, from between which proceed these words written in a roule, DE LE MALA QVE FECI, that is to say, Blot out the evils that I have done.

On the other side on the left hand, is Saint Peter with his Key, clothed in reddish yellow, holding his hand upon a woman clad in a gown of orange colour, which is on her knees, representing to the life Perrenelle, which holdeth her hands joined together, having a roule where is written, CHRISTE PRECOR ESTO PIVS, that is, Christ I beseech thee be pitiful: Behind whom there is an Angel on his knees, with a roule, that saith, SALVE DOMINE ANGELORVM, that is, All hail thou Lord of Angels. There is also another Angel on his knees, behind my Image, on the same side that St. Paul is on, which likewise holdeth a roule, saying, O REX SEMPITERNE, that is, O King everlasting. All this is so clear, according to the explication of the Resurrection and future judgement, that it may easily be fitted thereto. So it seems this Arch was not painted for any other purpose, but to represent this. And therefore we need not stay any longer upon it, considering that the least and most ignorant, may well know how to give this interpretation.

Next after the three that are rising again, come two Angels more of an Orange colour upon a blue field, saying in the roules, SVRGITE MORTVIVENITE AD IVDICIVM DOMINI MEI, that is, Arise you dead, come to the Judgement of my Lord. This also serves to the interpretation of the Resurrection: As also the last Figures following, which are, A man red vermillion, upon a field of Violet colour, who holdeth the foot of a winged Lion, painted of red vermillion also, opening his throat, as it were to devour the man : For one may say that this is the Figure of an unhappy sinner, who sleeping in a Lethargy of his corruption and vices, dieth without repentance and confession; who without doubt in this terrible Day shall be delivered to the Devil, here painted in form of a red roaring Lion, which will swallow and devour him.

CHAPTER II
The interpretations Philosophical, according to the Maistery of Hermes.

I desire with all my heart that he who searcheth the secrets of the Sages, having in his Spirit passed over these Ideas of the life and resurrection to come, should first make his profit of them : And in the second place, that he be more advised than before, that he sound and search the depth of my Figures, colours, and rowles; principally of my rowles, because that in this Art they speak not vulgarly. Afterward let him ask of himself why the Figure of Saint Paul is on the right hand, in the place where the custom is to paint S. Peter? And on the other side that of Saint Peter, in the place of the figure of Saint Paul? Why the Figure of Saint Paul is clothed in colours white and yellow, and that of S. Peter in yellow and red?

Why also the man and the woman which are at the feet of these two Saints praying to God, as if it were at the Day of Judgement, are apparelled in divers colours and not naked, or else nothing but bones, like them that are rising again? Why in this Day of Judgement they have painted this man and this woman at the feet of the Saints? For they ought to have been more low on earth, and not in heaven.

Why also the two Angels in Orange colour, which say in their rowles, SVRGITE MORTVI, VENITE AD IVDICIVM DOMINI MEI, that is Arise you dead, come unto the Judgement of my Lord, are clad in this colour, and out of their place, for they ought to be on high in heaven, with the two other which play upon the Instruments? Why they have a field Violet and blue? But principally why their roule, which speaks to the dead, ends in the open throat of the red and flying Lion?

I would then that after these, and many other questions which may justly be made, opening wide the eyes of his spirit, he come to conclude, that all this, not having been done without cause, there must be represented under this bark, some great secrets, which he ought to pray God to discover unto him. Having then brought his belief by degrees to this pass wish also that he would further believe, that these figures and explications are not made for them that have never seen the Books of the Philosophers, and who not knowing the Metallic principles, cannot be named Children of this Science; for if they think to understand perfectly these figures, being ignorant of the first Agent, they will undoubtedly deceive themselves, and never be able to know any thing at all.

Let no man therefore blame me, if he do not easily understand me, for he will be more blame-worthy than I, inasmuch as not being initiated into these sacred and secret interpretations of the first Agent, (which is the key opening the gates of all Sciences) he would notwithstanding, comprehend the most subtile conceptions of the envious Philosophers, which are not written but for them who already know these principles, which are never found in any book, because they leave them unto God, who revealeth them to whom he please, or else causeth them to be taught by the living voice of a Maister, by Cabalistical tradition, which happeneth very seldom.

Now then, my Son, let me so call thee, both because I am now come to a great age, and also for that, it may be, thou art otherwise a child of this knowledge, (God enable thee to learn, and after to work to his glory). Hearken unto me then attentively, but pass no further if thou be ignorant of the foresaid Principles.

This Vessel of earth, in this form, is called by the Philosophers, their triple Vessel, for within it there is in the middest a Stage, or a floor, and upon that a dish or a platter full of lukewarm ashes, within which is set the Philosophical Egg, that is, a vial of glass full of confections of Art (as of the feumme of the red sea, and the fat of the mercurial wind) which thou see painted in form of a Penner and Inkehorn. Now this Vessel of earth is open above to put in the dish and the vial, under which by the open gate, is put in the Philosophical fire, as thou knowest. So thou hast three vessels; and the threefold vessel: The envious have called an Athanor, a fiue, dung, Balneum Marie, a Furnace, a Sphere, the greene Lion, a prison, a grave, a urinal, a phioll, and a Bolts-head : I myself in my Summary or Abridgement of Philosophy, which I composed four years and two months past, in the end thereof named it the house and habitation of the Poulet, and the ashes of the Platter, the chaffe of the Poulet;

The common name is an Oven, which I should never have found, if Abraham the Jew had not painted it, together with the fire proportionable, wherein consists a great part of the secret. For it is as it were the belly, or the womb, containing the true natural heat to animate our young King : If this fire be not measured Clibanically, saith Calid the Persian, son of Iasichus; If it be kindled with a sword, saith Pithagoras; If thou fire thy Vessel, saith Morien, and maketh it feel the heat of the fire, it will give thee a box on the care, and burn his flowers before they be risen from the depth of his Marrow, making them come out red, rather than white, and then thy work is spoiled ; as also if thou make too little fire, for then thou shalt never see the end, because of the coldness of the natures, which shall not have had motion sufficient to digest them together.

The heat then of thy fire in this vessel, shall be (as saith Hermes and Rofinus) according to the Winter; or rather, as saith Diomedes, according to the heat of a Bird, which begins to fly so softly from the sign of Aries to that of Cancer : for know that the Infant at the beginning is full of cold phlegm and of milk, and that too vehement heat is an enemy of the cold and moisture of our Embrion, and that the two enemies, that is to say, our two elements of cold and heat will never perfectly embrace one another, but by little and little, having first long dwelt together, in the middest of the temperate heat of their bath, and being changed by long decoction, into Sulphur incombustible.

Govern therefore sweetly with equality and proportion, thy proud and haughty natures, for fear lest if thou favour one more than another, they which naturally are enemies, do grow angry against thee through jealousy, and dry Choller, and make thee sigh for it a long time after.

Besides this, thou must entertain them in this temperate heat perpetually, that is to say, night and day until the time that Winter, the time of the moisture of the matters, be passed; because they make their peace, and join hands in being heated together, whereas should these natures find themselves but one only half hour without fire, they would become for ever irreconcilable.

See therefore the reason why it is said in the Book of the seventy precepts: Look that their heat continue indefatigably without ceasing, and that none of their days be forgotten. And Rafis, the haste, saith he, that brings with it too much fire, is always followed by the Diuell, and Error. When the golden Bird, saith Diomedes, shall become just to Cancer, and that from thence it shall run toward Libra, then thou mayst augment the fire a little. And in like manner, when this faire Bird, shall fly from Libra towards Capricorn, which is the desired Autumn, the time of harvest, and of the fruits that are now ripe.

CHAPTER III

The two Dragons of colour yellowish, blue, and black like the field.

Look well upon these two Dragons, for they are the true principles or beginnings of this Philosophy, which the Sages have not dared to show to their own Children. He which is undermost, without wings, he is the fixed, or the male; that which is uppermost, is the volatile, or the female, black and obscure, which goes about to get the domination for many months. The first is called Sulphur, or heat and dryness, and the latter Argent vive, or cold and moisture. These are the Sun and Moon of the Mercurial source, and sulphurous original, which by continual fire are adorned with royal habiliments, that being united, and afterward changed into a quintessence, they may overcome every thing Metallic, how solid hard and strong, soever it be.

These are the Serpents and Dragons which the ancient AEgyptians have painted in a Circle, the head biting the tail, to signify that they proceeded from one and the same thing, and that it alone was sufficient, and that in the turning and circulation thereof, it made it self perfect : These are the Dragons which the ancient Poets have fained did without sleeping keep & watch the golden Apples of the Gardens of the Virgins Hesperides. These are they upon whom Jason in his adventure for the Golden Fleece, powred the broth or liquor prepared by the fair Medea, of the discourse of whom the Books of the Philosophers are so full, that there is no philosopher that ever was, but he hath written of it, from the time of the truth-telling hermes Trismegistus, Orpheus, Morienus, and the other following, even unto myself.

These are the two Serpents, given and sent by Juno, (that is, the nature Metallic) the which the strong Hercules, that is to say, the sage and wise man must strangle in his cradle, that is, overcome and kill them, to make them putrify, corrupt, and ingender, at the beginning of his work. These are the two Serpents, wrapped and twisted round about the Caduceus or rod of Mercury, with the which he exerciseth his great power, and transformeth himself as he lifteth. He, saith Haly, that shall kill the one, shall also kill the other, because the one cannot die, but with his brother.

These two then, (which Auicen calleth the Corassene bitch and the Armenian dog) these two I say, being put together in the vessel of the Sepulcher, do bite one another cruelly, and by their great poison, and furious rage, they never leave one another, from the moment that they have seized on one another (if the cold hinder them not) till both of them by their slavering venom, and mortal hurts, all of a goare bloud, over all the parts of their bodies; and finally, killing one another, be stewed in their proper venom, which after their death, changeth them into living and permanent water; before which time, they loose in their corruption and putrifaction, their first natural forms, to take afterwards one only new, more noble, and better form. These are the two Spermes, masculine and feminine, described at the beginning of my Abridgment of Philosophy, which are engendred (say Rafis, Auicen, and Abraham the Jew) within the Reynes, and entrails, and of the operations of the four Elements.

These are the radical moisture of metals, Sulphur and Argent Vive not vulgar, and such as are sold by the Merchants and Apothecaries, but those which give us those two fair and dear bodies which we love so much. These two spermes, saith Democritus, are not found upon the earth of the living: The same, saith Auicen, but he addeth, that they gather them from the dung, ordure, and rotteness of the Sun and Moon. O happy are they that know how to gather them; for of them they afterwards make a triacle, which hath power over all griefs, maladies, sorrows, infirmities, and weaknesses, and which fighteth puissantly against death, lengthening the life, according to the permission of God, even to the time determined, triumphing over the miseries of this world, and filling a man with the riches thereof.

Of these two Dragons or Principles Metallic, I have said in my fore-alledged Summary, that the Enemy would by his heat inflame his enemy, and that then if they take not heed, they should see in the air a venomous fume and a stinking, work in flame, and in poison, than the envenomed head of a Serpent, and Babylonian Dragon. The cause why I have painted these two spermes in the form of Dragons, is because their stench is exceeding great, and like the stench of them, and the exhalations which arise within the glass, are dark, black, blue, and yellowish (like as these two Dragons are painted) the force of which, and of the bodies dissolved, is so venomous, that truly there is not in the world a ranker poison; for it is able by the force and stench thereof, to mortify and kill everything living. The Philosopher never feels this stench, if he break not his vessels, but only he judgeth it to be such, by the sight, and the changing of colours, proceeding from the rottenness of his confections.

These colours then signify the putrifaction and generation which is given us, by the biting and dissolution of our perfect bodies, which dissolution proceedeth from external heat adding, and from the Pontique fierieness, and admirable sharp vertue of the poison of our Mercury, which maketh and resolveth into a pure cloud, that is, into impalpable powder, all that which it finds to resist it. So the heat working upon and against the radical, metallic, viscous, or oily moisture, ingendereth upon the subject, blackness. For at the same time the Matter is dissolved, is corrupted, groweth black, and conceiveth to ingender; for all corruption is generation, and therefore ought blackness to be much disired; for that is the black sail with the which the Ship of Theseus came back victorious from Crete, which was the cause of the death of his Father; so must this father die, to the intent, that from the ashes of this Phoenix another may spring, and that the son may be King.

Assuredly he that seeth not this blackness at the beginning of his operations, during the days of the Stone; what other colour soever he see, he shall altogether fail in the Maistery, and can do no more with that Chaos: for he works not well, if he putrify not; because if he do not putrify, he doeth not corrupt, nor ingender, and by consequence, the Stone cannot take vegetative life to increase and multiply.

And in all truth, I tell thee again, that though thou work upon the true matter, if at the beginning, after thou hast put they Confections in the Philosophers Egg, that is to say, sometime after the fire have stirred them up, if then, I say, thou seest not this head of the Crow, the black of the blackest black, thou must begin again, for this fault is irreparable, and not to be amended; especially the Orange colour, or half red, is to be feared, for if at the beginning thou see that in thine Egg, without doubt, thou burnest, or hast burnt the verdure and jueliness of thy Stone.

The colour which thou must have, ought to be intirely perfected in Blackness, like to that of these Dragons in the space of forty days: Let them therefore which shall not have these essential marks, retire themselves betimes from their operations, that they may redeem themselves from assured loss. Know also, and note it well, that in this Art it is but nothing to have this blackness, there is nothing more easy to come by: for from almost all things in the world, mixed with moisture, thou mayest have a blackness by the fire: but thou must have a blackness which comes from the perfect Metallic bodies, which lasts a long space of time, and is not destroyed in less than five months, after the which followeth immediately the desired whiteness. If thou hast this, thou hast enough, but not all. As for the colour blueish and yellowish, that signifieth that Solution and Putrefaction is not yet finished, and that the colours of our Mercury are not as yet well mingled, and rotten with the rest. Then this blackness, and these colours, teach plainly, that in this beginning the matter, and compound begins to rot and dissolve into powder, less than the Atoms of the Sun, the which afterwards are changed into coator permanent.

And this dissolution is by the envious Philosophers called Death, Destruction, and Perdition, because that the natures change their form, and from hence are proceeded so many Allegories of dead men, tombs and sepulchres. Others have called it Calcinatin, Denudation, Separation, Erituration, and Assation, because the Confections are changed and reduced into most small pieces and parts. Others have called it Reduction into the first matter, Mollification, Extraction, Commixtion, Liquefaction, Conversion of Elements, Subtiliation, Division, Humation, Impastation, and Distiliation, because that the Confections are melted, brought back into seed, softened, and circulated within the glass.

Others have called it Xir, or Iris, Putrefaction , Corruption, Cymmerian darkness, a gulf, Hell, Dragons, Generation, Ingression, Submersion, Completion, Conjunction, and Impregnation, because that the matter is black and waterish, and that the natures are prefectly mingled, and hold one of another. For when the heat of the Sun worketh upon them, they are changed, first into powder, or fat and glutinous water, which feeling the heat, flyeth on high to the poulets head, with the smoke, that is to say, with the wind and air; for thence this water melted, and drawn out of the confections, goeth down again, and in descending reduceth, and resolveth, as much as it can, the rest of the Aromatical confections, always doing so, until the whole be like a black broth somewhat fat. Now you see why they call this sublimation and volatization, because it flyeth on high, and Ascension and Descension, because it mounteth and descendeth within the glass.

A while after, the water beginneth to thicken and coagulate somewhat more, growing very black, like unto pitch, and finally comes the body and earth, which the envious have called Terra Foetida, that is, stinking earth: for then because of the perfect putrefaction, which is as natural as any other can be, this earth stinks, and gives a smell like the odour of graves filled with rottenness, and with bodies as yet charged with their natural moisture. This earth was by Hermes called Terra foliata, or the Earth of leaves, yet his true and proper name is Leton, which must afterward be whitened. The Ancient Sages that were Cabalists, have described it in their Metamorphoses, under the History of the Serpent of Mars, which had devoured the companions of Cadmus, who slew him, piercing him with his lance against a hollow Oak. Note this Oak.

CHAPTER IV

Of the man and the woman clothed in a gown of Orange colour
upon a field azure and blue, and of their rowles.

The man painted here doth expressly resemble myself to the natural, as the woman doth lively figure Perrenelle. The cause why we are painted to the life, is not particular to this purpose for it needed but to represent a male and a female, to the which our two particular resemblance was not necessarily required, but it pleased the Painter to put us there, just as he hath done higher in this Arch, at the feet of the Figure of Saint Paul and Saint Peter, according to that we were in our youth; as he hath likewise done in other places, as over the door of the Chapel of Saint James in the Bouchery near to my house (although that for this last there is a particular cause) as also over the door of Saincte Geneviesue des Ardans, where thou mayst see me. I made then to be painted here two bodies, one of a Male, and another of a Female, to teach thee that in this second operation, thou hast truely, but yet not perfectly, two natures conjoined and married together, the Masculine and the Feminine, or rather the four Elements; and that the four natural enemies, the hot and cold, dry and moist, begin to approach amiably one towards another, and by means of the Mediators and Peace-makers, lay down by little and little, the ancient enmity of the old Chaos.

Thou knowest well enough who these Mediators and Peace-makers are, between the hot and the cold there is moisture, for he is kinsman and allied to them both; to hot by his heat, and to cold by his

41

moisture: And this is the reason, why to begin to make this peace, thou hast already in the precedent operation, converted all the confections into water by dissolution. And afterward thou hast made to coagulate the water, which is turned into this Earth, black of the black most black, wholly to accomplish this peace; for the Earth, which is cold and dry, finding himself of kindred and alliance with the dry and moist, which are enemies, will wholly appease and accord them.

Doest thou not then consider a most perfect mixture of all the four Elements, having first turned them to water, and now into Earth? I will also teach thee hereafter the other conversions, into air when it shall be all white, and into fire, when it shall be of a most perfect purple. Then thou hast here two natures married together, whereof the one hath conceived by the other, and by this conception it is turned into the body of the Male, and the Male into that of the Female; that is to say, they are made one only body, which is the Androgyne or hermaphrodite of the Ancients, which they have also called otherwise the head of the Crow, or natures converted.

In this fashion I paint them here, because thou hast two natures reconciled, which (if they be guided and governed wisely) can form an Embrion in the womb of the Vessel, and afterwards bring forth a most puissant King, invincible and incorruptible, because it will be an admirable quintessence. Thus thou seest the principal and most necessary reason of this representation: The second cause, which is also well to be noted, was because I must of necessity paint two bodies, because in this operation it behoveth that thou divide that which hath been coagulated, to give afterwards nourishment, which is milk of life, to the little Infant when it is born, which is endued, by the living God, with a vegetable soul.

This is a secret most admirable and secret, which for want of understanding, it hath made fools of all those that have sought it without finding it, and hath made every man wise that beholds it with the eyes of his body, or of his spirit.

Thou must then make two parts and portions of this Coagulated body, the one of which shall serve for Azoth, to wash and cleanse the other, which is called Letch, which must be whitened: He which is washed is the Serpent Python, which, having taken his being from the corruption of the slime of the Earth gathered together by the waters of the deluge, when all the confections were water, must be killed and overcome by the arrows of the God Apollo, by the yellow Sun, that is to say, by our fire, equal to that of the Sun.

He which washeth, or rather the washings which must be continued with the other moity; these are the teeth of that Serpent, which the sage workman, the valiant Theseus, will sow in the same Earth, from whence there shall spring up armed Soldiers, which shall in the end discomfit themselves, suffering themselves by opposition to resolve into the same nature of the Earth, and the workman to bear away his deserved conquests.

It is of this that the Philosophers have written so often, and so often repeated it. It dissolves itself, it congeals itself, it makes itself black, it makes itself white, it kills itself, and it quickens itself. I have made their field be painted azure and blue, to show that I do but now begin to get out from the most black blackness, for the azure and blue is one of the first colours, that the dark woman lets us see, that is to say, moisture giving place a little to heat and dryness: The man and woman are almost all orange-coloured, to show that our Bodies, or our body which the wise men here call Rebis, hath not as yet digestion enough and that the moisture from whence comes the black blue and azure, is but half vanquished by the dryness.

For when dryness bears rule, all will be white, and when it fighteth with, or is equal to the moisture, all will be in part according to these present colours. The envious have also called these confections in this operation, Nummus, Ethelia, Arena, Boritis, Corfufle, Cambar, Albar aris, Duenech, Randeric, Kukul, Thabricis, Ebisemech, Ixir, &c which they have commanded to make white.

The woman hath a white circle in form of a rowle round about her body, to show thee that Rebis will begin to become white in that very fashion, beginning first at the extremities, round about this white circle. Scala Phylosophoru, that is the Book entitled The Philosophers Ladder, saith thus: The figure of the first perfect whiteness is the manifestation of a certain little circle of hair, that is passing over the head, which will appear on the sides of the vessels round about the matter, in a kind of a cierine or yellowish colour.

There is written in their Rowles, Home veniet ad judicium Dei, that is, Man shall come to the judgement of God : Vere (saith the woman) illa dies terribilis erit, that is, Truly that will be a terrible day. These are not passages of holy Scripture, but only sayings which speak according to the Theological sense, of the judgement to come. I have put them there to serve myself of them towards him, that beholds only the gross outward and most natural Artifice, taking the interpretation thereof to concern only the Resurrection, and also it may serve for them that gathering together the Parables of the Science, take to them the eyes of Lynceus, to pierce deeper then the visible objects. There is then, Man shall come to the judgement of God: Certainly that day shall be terrible. That is as if I should have said; It behoves that this come to the colour of perfection, to be judged and cleansed from all his blackness and filth, and to be spiritualized and whitened. Surely that day will be terrible, yet certainly, as you shall find in the Allegory of Aristeau, Horror holds us in prison by the space of four-score days, in the darkness of the waters, in the extreme heat of the Summer, and in the troubles of the Sea. All which things ought first to pass before our King can become white, coming from death to life, to overcome afterwards all his enemies.

To make thee understand yet somewhat better this Albification, which is harder and more difficult than all the rest, for till that time thou mayest err at every step, but afterwards thou canst not, except thou break thy vessels, I have also made for thee this Table following.

CHAPTER V

The figure of a man, like that of Saint Paul, clothed with a robe white and yellow, bordered with gold, holding a naked sword, having at his feet a man on his knees, clad in a robe of orange colour, black and white, holding a roule.

Mark well this man in the form of Saint Paul, clothed in a robe entirely of a yellowish white. If thou consider him well, he turns his body in such a posture, as shows that he would take the naked Sword, either to cut off the head, or to do some other thing, to that man which is on his knees at his feet, clothed in a robe of orange colour, white and black, which saith in his roule, DE LE MALA QVAE FECI, that is, Blot out all the evil which I have done, as if he should say, TOLLE NIGREDINEM, Take away from me my blackness; A term of Art: for Evil signifieth in the Allegory blackness, as it is often found in Turba Phylosophorum: Seeth it until it come to blackness, which will be thought Evil. But wouldest thou know what is meant by this man, that taketh the Sword? It signifies that thou must cut off the head of the Crow, that is to say, of the man clothed in divers Colours, which is on his knees.

I have taken this portrait and figure out of Hermes Trismagistus, in his Book of the Secret Art, where he saith, Take away the head of this black man, cut off the head of the Crow, that is to say, Whiten our black. Lambspring, that noble German, hath also used it in the Commentary of his Hieroglyphics, saying, In this wood there is a Beast all covered with black, if any man cut off his head, he will loose his blackness and put on a most white colour. Will you understand what that is? The blackness is called the head of the Crow, the which being taken away, at the instant comes the white colour: Then that is to say, when the Cloud appears no more, this body is said to be without a head.

These are his proper words. In the same sense the Sages have also said in other places, Take the Viper which is called De rexa, cut off his head, &c. that is to say, take away from him his blackness. They have also used this Periphrasis when to signify the multiplication of the Stone, they have fained a Serpent Hydra, whereof, if one cut off one head, there will spring in the place thereof ten; for the stone augments tenfold, every time that they cut off this head of the Crow, that they make it black, and afterwards white, that is to say, that they dissolve it anew, and afterward coagulate it again.

Mark how this naked Sword is wreathed about with a black girdle, and that the ends thereof are not so wreathed at all. This naked shining Sword is the stone for the white, or the white stone, so often by the Philosophers described under this form. To come then to this perfect and sparkling whiteness, thou must understand the wreathings of this black girdle, and follow that which they teach, which is the quantity of the imbibitions. The two ends which are not wreathed about at all, represent the beginning and the ending: for the beginning it teacheth that you must inbibe it at the first time gently and scarcely, giving it then a little milk, as to a little Child newborn, to the intent that Ifir, as the Authors say, be not drowned: The like must we do at the end, when we see that our King is full, and will have no more. The middle of these operations is painted by the five whole wreathes, or rounds, of the black girdle, at what time, (because our Salamander lives of the fire, and in the middest of the fire, and indeed is a fire, and an Argent vive, or quicksilver, that runs in the middest of the fire fearing nothing), thou must give him abundantly, in such sort that the Virgins Milk compass all the matter round about.

I have made to be painted black all these wreaths or rounds of the girdle, because these are the imbibitions, and by consequence, blacknesses: for the fire with the moisture (as it hath been often said) causeth blackness. And as these five whole wreathes or rounds show that you must do this five times wholly, so likewise they let you know that you must do this in five whole months, a month to every imbibition: See here the reason why Haly Abenragel said, the Coction or boiling of the things is done in three times fifty days: It is true that if thou count these little imbibitions at the beginning and at the end, there are seven. Whereupon one of the most envious hath said, Our head of the Crow is leprous, and therefore he that would cleanse it, he must make it go down seven times into the River of regeneration of Jordan, as the Prophet commanded the leprous Naaman the Syrian.

Comprehending herein the beginning, which is but of a few days, the middle, and the end, which is also very short. I have then given thee this table, to tell thee that thou must whiten my body, which is upon the knees, and demandeth no other thing: for Nature always tends to perfection, which thou shalt accomplish by the apposition of Virgins milk, and by the decoction of the matters which thou shalt make with this milk, which being dried upon this body, will colour it into this same white yellow, which he who takes the Sword, is clothed withall, in which colour thou must make they Corfufle to come. The vestments of the figure of Saint Paul are bordered largely with a golden and red citrine colour.

Oh my Son, praise God, if ever thou seest this, for now hast thou obtained mercy from Heaven; Imbibe it then, and teine it till such time as the little Infant be hardy ans strong, to combat against the water and the fire: In accomplishing the which, thou shalt do that which Demagoras, Senior, and Haly have called, The putting of the Mother into the Infants belly, which Infant the Mother had but lately brought forth; for they call the Mother the Mercury of Philosophers, wherewith they make their imbibitions and fermentations, and the Infant they call the Body, to teine or colour the which this Mercury is gone out. Therefore I have given thee these two figures, to signify the Albifications, for in this place it is that thou hast need of great help, for here all the World is deceived.

This operation is indeed a Labyrinth, for here there present themselves a thousand ways at the same instant, besides that, thou must go to the end of it, directly contrary to the beginning, in coagulating that which before thou dissolvedst, and in making earth that which before thou madest water. When thou hast made it white, then hast thou overcome the enchanted Bulls that cast fire and smoke out of their nostrils. Hercules hath cleansed the stable full of ordure, of rottenness, and of blackness. Jason hath powred the decoction or broth upon the

Dragons of Colchos, and thou hast in thy power the horn of Amalthea which (although it be white) may fill thee all the rest of thy life with glory, honour, and riches. To have the which, it hath behoved thee to fight valiantly, and in manner of an Hercules, for this Achelous, this moist river, is indewed with a most mighty force, besides that he often transfigures himself from one form to another. Thus hast thou done all, because the rest is without difficulty.

These transfigurations are particularly described in the Book of the Seven Egyptian Seals, where it is said (as also by all Authors) that the Stone, before it will wholly forsake his blackness, and become white in the fashion of a most shining marble, and of a naked flaming sword, will put on all the colours that thou canst possibly imagine, often will it melt, and often coagulate itself, and amidst these divers and contrary operations (which the vegetable soul which is in it makes it perform at one and the same time) it will grow Citrine, green, red (but not of a true red) it will become yellow, blue, and orange colour, until that being wholly overcome by dryness and heat, all these infinite colours will end in this admirable Citrine whiteness, of the colour of Saint Pauls garments, which in a short time will become like the colour of the naked sword; afterwards by the means of a more strong and long decoction it will take in the end a red Citrine colour, and afterward the perfect red of the vermillion, where it will repose itself forever.

I will not forget, by the way, to advertise thee, that the milk of the Moon, is not as the Virgins milk of the Sun; think then that the inibitions of whiteness, require a more white milk than those of a golden redness; for in this passage I had thought I should have missed, and so I had done indeed had it not been for Abraham the Jew; for this reason I have made to be painted for thee the Figure which taketh the naked sword, in the colour which is necessary for thee, for it is the Figure of that which whiteneth.

CHAPTER VI

Upon a green field, three resuscitants, or which rise again, two men and one woman, altogether white: Two Angels beneath, and over the Angels the figure of our Saviour coming to judge the world, clothed with a robe which is perfectly Citrine white.

I have so made to be painted for thee a field vert, because that in this decoction the confections become green, and keep this colour longer than any other after the black. This greenness shows particularly that our Stone hath a vegetable soul, and that by the Industry of Art it is turned into a true and pure tree, to bud abundantly, and afterwards to bring forth infinite little sprigs and branches. O happy green (saith the Rosary) which doest produce all things, without thee nothing can increase, vegetate, nor multiply. The three folk rising again, clothed in sparkling white, represent the body, soul, and Spirit of our white Stone.

The philosophers do ordinarily use these terms of Art to hide the secret from evil men. They call the Body that black earth, obscure and dark, which we make white: They call the Soul the other half divided from the Body, which by the will of God, and power of nature, gives to the body by his inibitions and fermentations a vegetable soul, that is to say, power and vertue to bud, encrease, multiply, and to become white, as a naked shining sword: They call the Spirit, the tincture & dryness, which as a Spirit hath power to pierce all Metallic things. I should be too tedious, if I should show thee how good reason they had to say always and in all places, Our Stone hath semblably to a man, a Body, Soul, and Spirit. I would only that thou note well, that as a man indued with a Body, Soul and Spirit, is notwithstanding but one, so likewise thou hast now but one only white confection, in the which nevertheless there are a Body, a Soul, and a Spirit, which are inseparably united.

I could easily give very clear comparisons and expositions of this Body, Soul, and Spirit; but to explicate them, I must of necessity speak things which God reserves to reveal unto them that fear and love him, and consequently ought not to be written. I have then made to be painted here, a Body, a Soul, and a Spirit, all white, as if they were rising again, to show thee, that the Sun and Moon and Mercury are raised again in this operation, that is to say, are made Elements of air, and whitened: for we have heretofore called the blackness, Death; and so continuing the Metaphor, we may call Whiteness, Life; which commeth not, but with, and by a Resurrection. The Body, to show this more plainly, I have made to be painted lifting up the stone of his tomb, wherein it was inclosed: The Soul, because it cannot be put into the earth, it comes not out of a tomb, but only I have made it be painted amongst the tombs, seeking its body, in form of a woman, having her hair dischevelled; The Spirit which likewise cannot be put in a grave, I have made to be painted in fashion of a man coming out of the earth, not from a Tomb. They are all white; so the blackness, that is death, is

50

vanquished, and they being whitened, are from henceforward incorruptible.

Now lift up thine eyes on high, and see our King coming, crowned and raised again, which hath overcome Death, the darknesses, and moistures; behold him in the form wherein our Saviour shall come, who shall eternally unite unto him all pure and clean souls, and will drive away all impurity and uncleanness, as being unworthy to be united to his divine Bidy. So by comparison (but first asking leave of the Catholic, Apostolic, and Roman Church, to speak in this manner, and praying every debonaire soul to permit me to use this similitude) see here our white Exilir, which from henceforward will inseparably unite unto himself every pure metallic nature, changing it into his own most fine silvery nature, rejecting all that is impure, strange, and Heterogeneal, or of another kind. Blessed be God, which of his goodness gives us grace to be able to consider this sparkling white, more perfect and shining than any compound nature, and more noble next after the immortal soul, than any substance having life, or not having life; for it is a quintessence, a most pure silver, that hath passed the Coppell, and is seven times refined, saith the royal Prophet David.

It is not needful to inperpret what the two Angels signify, that play on Instruments over the heads of them which are raised again: These are rather divine spirits, singing the mervails of God in this miraculous operation, than Angels that call to judgement. To make an express difference between these and them, I have given the one of them a Lute, the other a haultboy, but none of them trumpets, which yet are wont to be given to them that are to call us to Judgement. The like may be said of the three Angels, which are over the head of our Saviour, whereof the one crowneth him, and the other two assisting, say in their Rowles, O PATER OMNIPOTENS, O JESU BONE, that is, O Almighty Father, O good Jesu, in rendering unto him eternal thanks.

CHAPTER VII

Upon a field violet and blue, two Angels of an Orange colour, and their Rowles.

This violet and blue field showeth that being to pass from the white stone to the red, thou must inbibe it with a little virgins milk of the Sun, and that these colours come out of the Mercurial moisture which thou hast dried upon the Stone. In this operation of rubifying, although thou do imbibe, thou shalt not have much black, but of violets, blue and of the colour of the Peacocks tail. For our stone is so triumphant in dryness, that as soon as thy Mercury toucheth it, the nature thereof rejoicing in his like nature, it is joined unto it, and drinketh it greedily, and therefore the black that comes of moisture, can show itself but a little, and that under these colours violet and blue, because that dryness (as is said) doth by and by govern absolutely.

I have also made to be painted for thee, these two Angels with wings, to represent unto thee, that the two substances of thy confections, the Mercurial and the Sulphurous substance, the fixed as well as the volatile, being perfectly fixed together, do also fly together within thy vessel: for in this operation, the fixed body will gently mount to heaven, being all spiritual, and from thence it will descend unto the earth, and whethersoever thou wilt, following everywhere the Spirit, which is always moved upon the fire: Inasmuch as they are made one selfsame nature, and the compound is all spiritual, and the spiritual all corporall, so much hath it been subtilized upon our Marble, by the precedent operations. The natures then are here transmuted into Angels, that is to say, are made spiritual and most subtle, so are they now the true tinctures.

Now remember thee to begin the rubifying, by the apposition of Mercury Citrine red, but thou must not pour on much, and only once or twice, according as thou shalt see occasion; for this operation ought to be done by a dry fire, and by a dry sublimation and calcination. And truely I tell thee here a secret which thou shalt very seldom find written, so far am I from being envious, that would to God every man knew how to make gold to his own will, that they might live, and lead forth to pasture their fair flocks, without Usury or going to Law, in imitation of the holy Patriarchs using only (as our first Fathers did) to exchange one thing for another; and yet to have that, they must labour as well as now.

Howbeit for fear to offend God, and to be the instrument of such a change which prove evil, I must take heed to represent or write where it is that we hide the keys, which can open all the doors of the secrets of nature, or to open or cast up the earth in that place, contenting myself to show the things which will teach everyone to whom God shall give permission to know what property the sign of the Balance or Libra hath, when it is inlightened by the Sun and Mercury in the month of October.

These Angels are painted of an orange colour, to let thee know that thy white confections have been a little more digested, or boiled, and that the black of the violet and blue hath been already chafed away by the fire: for this orange colour is compounded of the fair golden Citrine red (which thou hast so long waited for) and of the remainder of this violet and blue, which thou hast already in part banished and undone. Furthermore this orange colour showeth that the natures are digested, and by little and little perfected by the grace of God.

As for their Rowle, which saith, SVRGITE MORTVI, VENITE AD IVDICIVM DOMINI MEI, that is, Arise you dead, and come unto the judgement of God my Lord; I have made it be put there, only for the Theological sense, rather than any other: It ends in the throat of a Lion which is all red, to teach that this operation must not be discontinued until they see the true red purple, wholly like unto the Poppy of the Hermitage, and the vermillion of the painted Lion saving for multiplying.

CHAPTER VIII

The figure of a man, like unto Saint Peter, clothed in a robe Citrine red, holding a key in his right hand, and laying his left hand upon a woman, in an orange coloured robe, which is on her knees at his feet, holding a rowle.

Look upon this woman clothed in a robe of orange colour, which doth so naturally resemble Perrenelle as she was in her youth; She is painted in the fashion of a suppliant upon her knees, her hands joined together, at the feet of a man which hath a key in his right hand, which hears her graciously, and afterwards stretcheth out his left hand upon her. Wouldest thou know what this meaneth? This is the Stone, which in this operation demandeth two things, of the Mercury of the Sun, of the Philosophers (painted under the form of a man) that is to say Multiplication, and a more rich Accoustrement; which at this time it is needful for her to obtain, and therefore the man so laying his hand upon her shoulder accords and grants it unto her. But why have I made to be painted a woman? I could as well have made to be painted a man as a woman, or an Angel rather, (for the whole natures are now spiritual and corporal, masculine and feminine), but I have rather chosen to cause paint a woman, to the end that thou mayest judge that she demands rather this than any other thing, because these are the most natural and proper desires of a woman.

To show further unto thee that she demandeth Multiplication, I have made paint the man, unto whom she addresseth her prayers in the form of Saint Peter, holding a key, having power to open and to shut, to bind and to loose, because the envious Philosophers have never spoken of Multiplication, but under the common terms of Art, APERI, CLAVDE, SOLVE, LIGA, that is, Open, shut, bind, loose, opening and loosing, they have called the making of the Body (which is always hard and fixt) soft fluid, and running like water: To shut and to bind, is with them afterwards by a more strong decoction to coagulate it, and to bring it back again into the form of a body.

It behoved me then, in this place to represent a man with a key, to teach thee that thou must now open and shut, that is to say, Multiply the budding and encreasing natures: for look how often thou shalt dissolve and fix, so often will these natures multiply, in quantity, quality, and vertue, according to the multiplication of ten; coming from this number to an hundred, from an hundred to a thousand, from a thousand to ten thousand, from ten thousand to an hundred thousand, from an hundred thousand to a million, and from thence by the same operation to Infinity, as I have done three times, praised be God. And when thy Elixir is so brought unto Infinity, one grain thereof falling upon a quantity of molten metal as deep and vast as the Ocean, it will teine it, and convert it into most perfect metal, that is to say, into silver or gold, according as it shall have been imbibed and fermented, expelling and drying out far from himself all the impure and strange matter, which was joined with the metal in the first coagulation: for this reason therefore have I made to be painted a Key in the hand of the man, which is in the form of Saint Peter, to signify that the stone desireth to be opened and shut for multiplication, and likewise to show thee with what Mercury thou oughtest to do this, & when; I have given the man a garment Citrine red, and the woman one of orange colour.

Let this suffice, lest I transgress the silence of Pythagoras, to teach thee that the woman, that is, our stone, asketh to have the rich Accoustrements and colour of Saint Peter. She hath written in her Rowle, CHRISTE PRECOR ESTO PIVS, that is, Jesu Christ be pitiful unto me, as if she said, Lord be good unto me, and suffer not that he that shall become thus far, should spoil all with too much fire: It is true, that from henceforward I shall no more fear mine enemies, and that all fire shall be alike unto me, yet the vessel that contains me, is always brittle and easy to be broken: for if they exalt the fire overmuch, it will crack and flying a pieces, will carry me and sow me unfortunately amongst the ashes.

Take heed therefore to thy fire in this place, and govern sweetly with patience, this admirable quintescence, for the fire must be augmented unto it, but not too much. And pray the soveraign Goodness, that it will not suffer the evil spirits which keep the Mines and Treasures, to destroy thy work, or to bewitch thy sight, when thou considereth these incomprehensible motions of this quintescence within thy vessel.

CHAPTER IX

Upon a dark violet field, a man red purple, holding the foot of a
Lion red as vermillion, which hath wings, for it seems would ravish and
carry away the man.

This field violet and dark, tells us that the stone hath obtained by
her full decoction, the fair Garments, that are wholly Citrine and red,
which she demanded of Saint Peter, who was clothed therewith, and
that her complete and perfect digestion (signified by the entire
Citrinity) hath made her leave her old robe of orange colour. The
vermilion red colour of this flying Lion, like the pure and clear scarlet
in grain, which is of the true Granadored, demonstrates that it is now
accomplished in all right and equality. And that she is now like a Lion,
devouring every pure metallic nature, and changing it into her true
substance, into true and pure gold, more fine than that of the best
mines.

Also she now carrieth this man out of this vale of miseries, that is
to say, out of the discommodities of poverty and infirmity, and with her
wings gloriously lifts him up, out of the dead and standing waters of
AEgypt, (which are the ordinary thoughts of mortal men) making him
despise this life and the riches thereof, and causing him night and day to
meditate on God, and his Saints, to swell in the Emperial heaven, and to
drink the sweet springs of the Fountains of everlasting hope.

Praised be God eternally, which hath given us grace to see this most fair and all-perfect purple colour; this pleasant colour of the wild poppy of the Rock, this Tyrian, sparkling and flaming colour, which is incapable of Alternation or change, over which the heaven itself, nor his Zodiac can have no more domination nor power, whose bright shining rays, that dazzle the eyes, seem as though they did communicate unto a man some supercelestial thing, making him (when he beholds and knows it) to be astonished, to tremble, and to be afraid at the same time.

Oh Lord, give us grace to use it well, to the augmentation of the Faith, to the profit of our Souls, and to the encrease of the glory of this noble Realm. Amen.

www.ingramcontent.com/pod-product-compliance
Lightning Source LLC
Chambersburg PA
CBHW071750090426
42738CB00011B/2632